Superstorm Sandy

OCTOBER 29, 2012

by Doug Sanders

Consultant: Michael J. Brennan, PhD
Meteorologist

BEARPORT PUBLISHING

New York, New York

Credits

Cover and Title Page, © Associated Press; TOC, © The Middletown Press; 4T, © Steve Earley/Associated Press; 4B, © NY Daily News via Getty Images; 5, © Getty Images; 6, © Charles Sykes/Associated Press; 7, © Associated Press; 8, © Alan Diaz/Associated Press; 9, © Miami Herald/Getty Images; 11, © Mark C. Olsen/ZUMA Press/Newscom; 12, © Allison Joyce/Getty Images; 13, © Associated Press; 14 © NY Daily News via Getty Images; 15, © Mark Lennihan/Associated Press; 16, © Monika Graff/UPI/Newscom; 17, © Adam Hunger/Reuters; 18, © Anthony Deprimo/Staten Island Advance/Landov; 19, © Mike Segar/Reuters; 20, © Seth Wenig/Associated Press; 21, © Shannon Stapleton/Reuters; 22, © iStockphoto/Thinkstock; 23T, © 2013 Gannett-CommNews; 23B, © Jim West/Alamy; 24, © FEMA/Walt Jennings; 25L, © Phil McAuliffe/Polaris/Newscom; 25R, © Anton Oparin/Shutterstock; 26, © FEMA/Liz Roll; 27, © Frances Roberts/Alamy; 28T, © NY Daily News via Getty Images; 28B, © Mike Segar/Reuters; 29T, © 2013 Gannett-CommNews; 29B, © Phil McAuliffe/Polaris/Newscom; 29BKG, © iStockphoto/Thinkstock; 30–31, © The Gazette.

Publisher: Kenn Goin
Senior Editor: Joyce Tavolacci
Creative Director: Spencer Brinker
Design: Dawn Beard Creative
Photo Researcher: We Research Pictures

Library of Congress Cataloging-in-Publication Data

Sanders, Doug, 1972– author.
   Superstorm Sandy / by Doug Sanders ; consultant, Michael J. Brennan, PhD, meteorologist.
      pages cm. — (Code red)
   Includes bibliographical references and index.
   ISBN-13: 978-1-61772-898-3 (library binding)
   ISBN-10: 1-61772-898-5 (library binding)
   1. Hurricane Sandy, 2012—Juvenile literature. 2. Hurricane damage—United States—Juvenile literature. 3. Hurricanes—United States—Juvenile literature. 4. Disaster relief—United States—Juvenile literature. I. Title. II. Series: Code red.
   QC944.2.S26 2014
   551.55'20974—dc23
                                         2013011498

For more information, write to Bearport Publishing Company, Inc., 45 West 21st Street, Suite 3B, New York, New York 10010. Printed in the United States of America.

10 9 8 7 6 5 4 3 2 1

Contents

A Close Call

It was October 29, 2012, in Howard Beach, New York. A massive **hurricane** named Sandy was hurtling toward the East Coast. The wind howled outside Aura Meza's seaside apartment, as the waves in the nearby ocean grew bigger and bigger. Then, like an explosion going off, the glass doors in the back of her apartment suddenly shattered. Aura turned to run into her living room, but there was no time. She was surrounded by water!

Hurricane Sandy making its way toward the East Coast

Aura Meza

Waves of cold water from the ocean had burst through the doors and were pouring into her apartment. "It was like a **tsunami**, it came from nowhere," Aura said. The water was now up to her chest and rising quickly. Her refrigerator was floating in the kitchen. The water covered her stove and popped her air conditioner out of the wall. Would Aura be able to escape to safety?

When Sandy hit, Howard Beach and hundreds of other communities along the East Coast became flooded with ocean water.

Hurricane Sandy is the largest Atlantic Ocean hurricane ever to hit the United States.

Making an Escape

When Superstorm Sandy arrived, it pushed millions of gallons of water from the ocean onto land along the East Coast. With the ocean now inside her apartment, Aura scooped up her dog, Tinker, from the chilly water. Glancing out her window, Aura saw water everywhere. She couldn't believe how powerful it was. "The water was pushing cars down the street," she said.

Water from the storm forces a car down a street in a New Jersey town not far from Howard Beach.

66 The water was moving everything. 99

—Aura Meza

With Tinker in her arms, Aura **waded** through her flooded apartment. She made her way to a higher floor in her building, where it was dry and safe. There she met a neighbor who noticed Aura had a deep cut on her right foot. Aura's foot was soon **bandaged**—but the storm's widespread destruction could not be so easily fixed.

Scientists rank hurricanes on a scale of 1 to 5 based on the strength of their winds. A Category 5 hurricane is the strongest. Even though Sandy was only a Category 1 when it struck the United States, it was still a very powerful storm due to its large size.

A flooded neighborhood near Aura's Howard Beach home

Birth of a Superstorm

By the time Sandy had flooded Aura's home, **meteorologists** had already been tracking the storm for about a week. It had started as a small **tropical storm** in the Caribbean Sea on October 22, 2012. At that time, meteorologists had named the storm Sandy.

A meteorologist tracks Sandy at the National Hurricane Center in Miami, Florida.

Each year, scientists name every tropical storm. The first storm gets a name starting with *A*, the next one's name begins with *B*, and so on. As Sandy was the nineteenth storm of the year, its name began with *S*, the nineteenth letter in the alphabet.

As the storm grew larger, it moved north, slamming into several Caribbean islands in its path. Sandy's strong winds ripped up trees. Heavy rains from the storm flooded houses and streets. Its powerful winds swirled faster and faster. Sandy had now become a hurricane. The storm continued north across the Atlantic Ocean—heading for the United States!

In Haiti, an island country in the Caribbean, the heavy rains from Sandy flooded homes and created dangerous mudslides.

Landfall!

As Sandy moved north, the storm grew bigger and stronger. Its 80-mile-per-hour (129 kph) winds whipped up the ocean, creating giant waves. The hurricane sped toward the New Jersey coast. A week after the storm began, it finally made **landfall** in the United States around 8:00 p.m. on October 29. As the storm moved onto land, it lost some of its strength. However, it would still leave a long trail of destruction in its path.

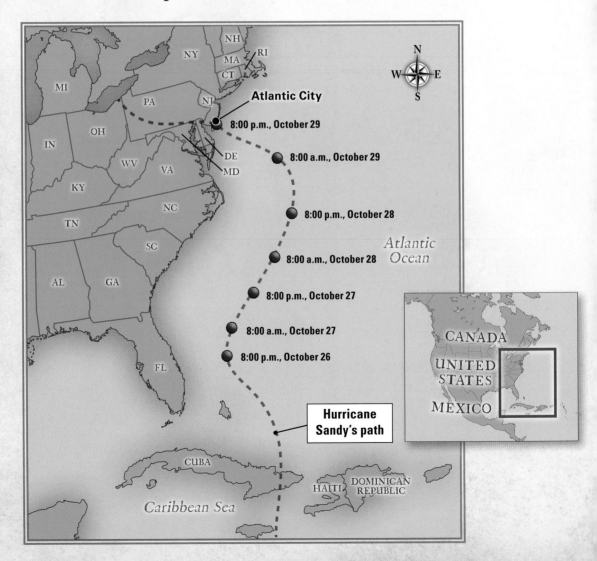

Atlantic City
8:00 p.m., October 29

8:00 a.m., October 29

8:00 p.m., October 28

Atlantic Ocean

8:00 a.m., October 28

8:00 p.m., October 27

8:00 a.m., October 27

8:00 p.m., October 26

Hurricane Sandy's path

CANADA

UNITED STATES

MEXICO

Caribbean Sea

CUBA

HAITI

DOMINICAN REPUBLIC

The storm had made landfall at **high tide**—when the ocean is at its highest level. As a result, Sandy's **storm surge** combined with the high tide caused huge waves of seawater to crash onto shore. The surge ripped up parts of the **boardwalk** along the shore of New Jersey, washing them away. The **floodwaters** also tore apart houses and spread **inland**, filling up basements and trapping people in their homes.

The flooded shoreline of Atlantic City during the start of the storm

Sandy made landfall about five miles (8 km) southwest of Atlantic City, New Jersey.

City Underwater

When Sandy hit land, the giant storm caused great destruction throughout a huge area of the northeastern United States. To the north of Atlantic City, floodwaters spilled onto low-lying areas of Manhattan. The rush of water from the ocean and nearby rivers flooded power stations and damaged electrical **equipment**, causing **blackouts**. Hundreds of thousands of people were left without power. Lower Manhattan, which was usually brightly lit up at night, was now completely dark.

Most of lower Manhattan lost power during the storm. People were forced to live without heat, hot water, lights, TV, cell phones, and computers.

Superstorm Sandy brought the city to a halt. Water flooded cars and streets. Highways looked like rivers. The surge had also filled **subway** tunnels with seawater, as well as other tunnels around the city. As a result, it became impossible for people to travel in some parts of Manhattan. At the entrance to the Brooklyn-Battery Tunnel in Manhattan, tow trucks used to remove broken-down cars became covered with water. Now the tow trucks were the ones in need of help.

A flooded subway station in New York City

The storm surge and the tide caused the water level to rise 14 feet (4.3 m) above normal in New York Harbor.

Flood and Fire

Flooding wasn't the only danger that victims of Sandy faced. While sections of Manhattan were underwater, the nearby neighborhood of Breezy Point, Queens, was facing a different type of threat—fire! A blaze began shortly after the hurricane damaged one home's electrical system, causing the house to catch on fire. In no time, the flames spread to nearby houses.

Flames spreading through the Breezy Point neighborhood

Firefighters tried to speed to the scene. However, because the streets were flooded, their trucks couldn't reach the fire right away. In addition, Sandy's winds fanned the flames and helped the fire grow. "The wind is pushing it [fire] from house to house," said firefighter Danny Glover. More than 190 firefighters fought for ten long hours to put out the blaze.

More than 100 homes in Breezy Point burned to the ground.

66It's awful. There's a lot of history in this place, and now it's all gone.99

–Matt Long, who lost his Breezy Point home in the fire

Swimming to Safety

In a different part of Queens, another firefighter was also battling the destruction caused by Sandy. "When I saw the water crashing against my basement windows," Brian Kelly said, "I knew this was serious." Belle Harbor, the neighborhood where Brian lived, was quickly filling with floodwaters.

A house and car in Belle Harbor, Queens, destroyed by the storm's floodwaters

66 I knew, as a firefighter who understands danger, that this was dead serious. 99

—Brian Kelly

Brian knew he had to act fast in order to save himself and his family from drowning. Using his training as a firefighter, he placed his three children on his back. He then waded through the rising water to a neighbor's house that had not flooded. Brian left his children with his neighbor and then went back for his wife. With the water now up to his chest, Brian carried her to safety. He had saved his family from the deadly storm.

A rescuer carries a boy on his back through Sandy's floodwaters.

Brian also saved his 78-year-old father-in-law from the flood. To save him, "I literally swam up through the surging chest-high waters of my street," said Brian.

Up a Tree

For the people caught in Sandy's path, the power of the storm was like nothing they had ever experienced. Lisa Perez, for example, was in her Staten Island home when she saw waves of floodwaters rushing up her street. Lisa ran outside to move her car to safety. Only a few steps from her car, the surge knocked her off her feet. She was swept into the flood. "I felt myself drowning," Lisa said.

Lisa's hometown of Oakwood Beach, Staten Island, after the storm

As Lisa yelled for help, she spotted her next-door neighbor Eddie. He was also trapped in the floodwaters. Eddie's eyes were drawn to a large tree between their two houses. "Go for the tree!" he shouted to Lisa. As the water rose even higher, Lisa and Eddie swam to the tree and climbed up it. They huddled together on a large branch until the storm died down.

Lisa and Eddie spent close to two hours in the tree during the most intense part of the storm before they were able to swim home.

66I never thought that tree would save my life one day.**99**

–Lisa Perez

Lisa Perez and her neighbor Eddie in front of the tree that saved them

After the Storm

Lisa Perez was able to return to her home, but she had no electricity or heat. She lit candles in her dark house and used extra blankets to stay warm through the cold night. The next morning, the storm was over. However, the destruction it had brought was not. The storm had damaged power stations and electrical equipment, leaving millions of people without electricity and heat.

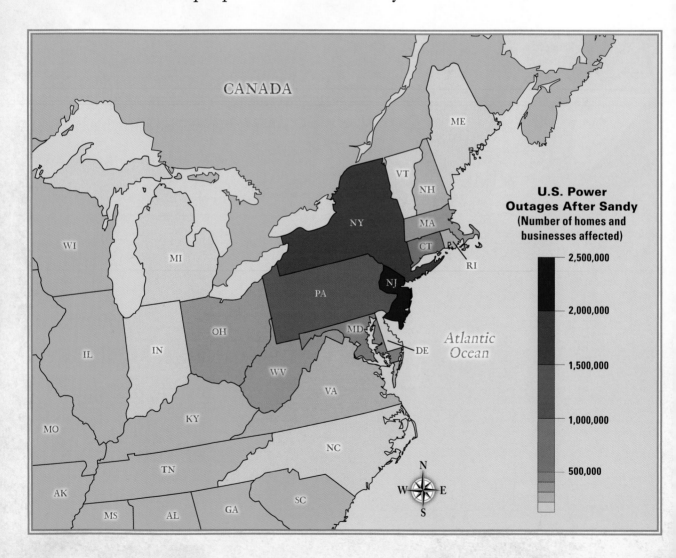

Sandy had devastated thousands of houses and other buildings in several states. After the storm, many people tried to return to their homes. Unfortunately, some discovered they had no homes to go back to. For example, in Far Rockaway, Queens, Nicole Abrams and her three daughters came back to a flooded mess. "The water came up from the basement all the way to the first floor," Nicole said. She and her family were left with no heat or hot water for several weeks. With colder weather arriving, Nicole had no choice but to find a new place to live.

The family who had lived in this home in Queens before the storm hit was forced to find a new place to live.

Superstorm Sandy caused 100 deaths and affected more than 50 million people.

❝I will not stay here any longer . . . to experience any more hurricanes.❞

–Nicole Abrams

Without a Home

Some families remained in their flooded homes. However, another problem soon appeared—mold. This **fungus** appears as black or green splotches and grows on damp surfaces. In some cases, mold can irritate people's lungs and make them sick. Mold spread throughout many homes damaged by Sandy's floodwaters. This forced the people living in them to **evacuate** and find new places to live.

Black mold growing in a home that had flooded

Mold is very common in homes and will grow anywhere there is moisture. It can usually be seen or smelled.

All along the East Coast, Superstorm Sandy **evacuees** were given temporary housing in hotels, shelters, and trailers. For example, Hope Ishmael and her children moved into a small hotel in Ocean Grove, New Jersey. Her apartment was badly damaged in the flood, so she and her family had to stay in the hotel until they found a new place to live. "They make it like home here," she said, "but there's nothing like your own kitchen and your own home."

Hope Ishmael was pregnant when the storm struck. She and her family were forced to spend Christmas away from home.

Hurricane Sandy survivors at a shelter receiving food

Help Arrives

Storms like Sandy have struck other parts of the country before. As a result, the government formed **FEMA** (Federal Emergency Management Agency) in 1979 to help people harmed by **natural disasters**. Among its many duties, FEMA helps disaster survivors find shelter and pay for home and business repairs.

A FEMA worker assists storm victims.

To help Sandy survivors, FEMA sent 1,693 workers to the storm area and set up more than 75 disaster recovery centers.

FEMA, however, was not the only source of help after Sandy hit. Friends and neighbors took in those without a home. Thousands of **volunteers** from across the country arrived with **donations** of food and clothing to help Sandy survivors. "I am really thankful for all the help we are getting from people," said Ronny Kmiotek, who lost his house in the storm.

After the floodwaters drained away, volunteers provided food and clothing to survivors.

New Jersey governor Chris Christie speaking in Seaside Heights, New Jersey

"It is beyond anything I thought I would ever see. Terrible. So we need to remain patient.**"**

–Chris Christie, governor of New Jersey

Looking to the Future

For many of the people who were left homeless after the storm, it was time to rebuild. In areas hit hard by the storm, it would take months to replace what had been destroyed.

Life after Sandy would never be the same. People living along the northeast coast now had a new problem to worry about: hurricanes. Sandy was the largest storm of its kind to strike the region. What if the next storm was even bigger?

A FEMA worker helps repair a house.

New York State needed more than $42 billion to recover from Sandy— $33 billion to repair houses and roads, and $9 billion to protect transportation and power systems from future storms.

Since Superstorm Sandy struck, people have learned how to be better prepared for hurricanes. Survivor Aura Meza now knows to evacuate when a powerful storm is on its way. Even though Sandy destroyed nearly everything she owned, Aura remains hopeful. "I don't look back," she said. "I have to look to the future."

Volunteers work together to clean up a boardwalk in Coney Island, New York, after Superstorm Sandy.

Many people showed great courage and compassion during and after Superstorm Sandy. Here are four of them.

Aura Meza was in her Howard Beach apartment when Sandy hit.

- Was forced to flee her apartment after it flooded
- Escaped to a higher floor in her building
- Suffered a deep cut on her foot
- Lost almost everything she owned
- Lived with family until her apartment was repaired

Lisa Perez was at home in Staten Island when her neighborhood flooded.

- Was swept away by Hurricane Sandy's floodwaters
- Survived by climbing a tree and waiting in the branches
- Was able to return home after the storm but did not have electricity or heat

Hope Ishmael was living in Red Bank, New Jersey, with her two children when her home was badly damaged by the storm.

- Was pregnant when the storm struck
- Was forced to move out of her apartment after it was damaged by floodwaters
- Lived at a small hotel with her children while her home was repaired

Chris Christie was the governor of New Jersey during Superstorm Sandy.

- Toured the worst-hit parts of New Jersey and helped organize relief efforts
- Worked with President Barack Obama to provide storm survivors with aid
- Met with and comforted survivors
- Helped rebuild towns damaged by the storm

Glossary

bandaged (BAN-dijd) wound pieces of cloth around an injured body part

blackouts (BLAK-*outs*) periods of time when the electricity in an area fails and the lights go out

boardwalk (BORD-wawk) a wooden walkway that borders a beach

donations (doh-NAY-shuhns) gifts of money or supplies to help people in need

equipment (i-KWIP-muhnt) the tools and machines needed to do a job

evacuate (i-VAK-yoo-ayt) to leave a dangerous place

evacuees (ee-*vak*-yew-EES) people forced to leave their homes, often due to a natural disaster

FEMA (FEE-muh) letters standing for Federal Emergency Management Agency; a U.S. government organization that helps communities prepare for and recover from disasters

floodwaters (FLUHD-*wa*-turz) water overflowing as a result of a flood

fungus (FUHN-guhss) a plant-like organism such as a mushroom that cannot make its own food

high tide (HYE TIDE) the time of day when the ocean comes up highest on the shore

hurricane (HUR-uh-*kayn*) a circular storm that forms over the ocean, with heavy rains and winds of at least 74 miles per hour (119 kph)

inland (IN-luhnd) on land; away from the water

landfall (LAND-fawl) the arrival of a hurricane onto dry land

meteorologists (*mee*-tee-ur-OL-oh-jists) scientists who study and predict the weather

natural disasters (NACH-ur-uhl duh-ZASS-turz) events caused by nature that result in great loss, hardship, and damage

storm surge (STORM SURJ) the rise of water due to a storm or hurricane

subway (SUHB-*way*) an electric train that runs underground

tropical storm (TROP-uh-kuhl STORM) a circular storm that forms over the ocean, with heavy rains and winds of between 39 and 73 miles per hour (63 and 117 kph)

tsunami (tsoo-NAH-mee) a huge wave or group of waves caused by an underwater earthquake

volunteers (*vol*-uhn-TEERS) people who help others and receive no payment in return

waded (WAYD-id) walked in or through shallow water

Bibliography

Barron, James. "After the Devastation, a Daunting Recovery."
The New York Times (October 30, 2012).

Federal Emergency Management Agency: http://www.fema.gov/sandy

National Geographic: news.nationalgeographic.com/news/2012/10/
pictures/hurricane-sandy-pictures-floods-fire-snow-in-the-aftermath/

Richardson, Clem. "Hurricane Sandy took almost all Aura Marina
Meza's possessions, but not her unshakeable faith." *Daily News*
(December 3, 2012).

Read More

Aronin, Miriam. *Mangled by a Hurricane! (Disaster Survivors).*
New York: Bearport (2010).

Gregory, Josh. *The Superstorm Hurricane Sandy (True Books).* New York:
Children's Press (2013).

Hojem, Benjamin. *Hurricanes: Weathering the Storm (All Aboard Science
Reader).* New York: Grosset & Dunlap (2010).

Learn More Online

To learn more about Superstorm Sandy, visit
www.bearportpublishing.com/CodeRed

Index

About the Author

Doug Sanders lives in New York City. He still has the
flashlight he used during the Hurricane Sandy power outage.